Little Bo-Peep

Joseph Martin Kronheim

[ZHINGOORA BOOKS]

Joseph Martin Kronheim

LITTLE BO-PEEP

This digital edition is published by Zhingoora Books.

The Cover is Designed by Pallav Sethiya.

zhingoora_books@yahoo.com

Joseph Martin Kronheim

LITTLE BO-PEEP

"Little Bo-Peep she lost her sheep
And didn't know where to find them.
Let them alone, and they'll come home,
And bring their tails behind them!"

Joseph Martin Kronheim

3

LITTLE BO-PEEP

Joseph Martin Kronheim

LITTLE BO-PEEP

So runs the *Nursery Rhyme*.
Little Bo-Peep was a very nice
little girl. Her cheeks had a bloom
on them like a lovely peach, and
her voice sounded like a sweet
silver bell.

But though Little Bo-Peep was as
good as she was beautiful, she
sometimes met with misfortunes
that made her very sad. Once,
when she lost her sheep, she was

Joseph Martin Kronheim

5

very doleful indeed. And this is how it happened.

One summer evening, when the sun was setting, Little Bo-Peep, who had to rise very early in the morning, felt tired, and sat down on a bank covered with daisies. Being very weary she soon fell fast asleep. Now the Bell-wether of Bo-Peep's flock was a most stupid and stubborn fellow. I dare say you know that all the sheep in

Joseph Martin Kronheim

6

LITTLE BO-PEEP

a flock will follow the Bell-wether,
and that he always wears a bell
round his neck. It was a great
pity, but the Bell-wether of Bo-
Peep's flock was very wild, and was
much given to wander far away into
the wood, where of course the rest
of the sheep would follow him.

Finding Little Bo-Peep asleep,
the tiresome fellow began by
standing on his hind legs and
making a great bow to his shadow

Joseph Martin Kronheim

before him on the grass. After
this he whirled himself round like a
top, shaking his head all the time,
and ringing his bell.

Joseph Martin Kronheim

8

LITTLE BO-PEEP

Joseph Martin Kronheim

LITTLE BO-PEEP

Very soon the rest of the flock
began to dance and caper too.
And when they had wheeled round
their leader for a time, they ran
off after him with a bound into the
wood. Away they went, till they
were quite tired out; and then
they came to a stand-still, staring
at their leader with very blank
faces. But the Bell-wether looked
foolish enough now, and did
nothing but shake his head slowly

Joseph Martin Kronheim

LITTLE BO-PEEP

and ring his bell, which seemed to
say quite clearly, "You are lost,
you are lost!"

When Little Bo-Peep awoke she
found her sheep gone, and hardly
knowing what she did, she walked
on and on, far into the wood. She
met some people with hoes and
rakes in their hands, and asked
them if they had seen her sheep.
But they only laughed at her, and
said, No. One man was very cross,

Joseph Martin Kronheim

and threatened to beat her. At last she came to a stile, on which an old Raven was perched. He looked so wise that Little Bo-Peep asked him whether he had seen a flock of sheep. But he only cried "Caw, caw, caw;" so Bo-Peep ran on again across the fields.

Joseph Martin Kronheim

LITTLE BO-PEEP

Joseph Martin Kronheim

LITTLE BO-PEEP

She wandered on till night-fall, and being faint with hunger, was very glad to see a light just before her. As she went on, she saw that it shone from a cottage window. But when she came to the door, it looked so dark and dismal that she was afraid to go in, and was just going to run away, when a cross-looking old woman came out, and dragged her into the cottage. She made her sit by the side of

Joseph Martin Kronheim

her son, who was a very ugly
youth with a great red face and
red hair.

Joseph Martin Kronheim

15

LITTLE BO-PEEP

Joseph Martin Kronheim

LITTLE BO-PEEP

The old woman told him that she had brought Bo-Peep to be his wife, so Bo-Peep, who did not like him at all, ran away while they were asleep. But she did not know where to go, and gave herself up for lost, when she heard something cry, "tu-whit——tu-whoo," in the tree above her. It was a great owl, which began flapping its wings with joy. Bo-Peep was frightened at first, but as the owl seemed

Joseph Martin Kronheim

very kind, she followed it. It took her to a cottage were there was plenty to eat and drink, and then, to Bo-Peep's great surprise, it began to speak, and told her this story:——

"Know, dear Maiden," said the owl, "that I am the daughter of a King, and was a lovely Princess; but I was changed into an owl by the old woman at the cottage, because I would not marry her

LITTLE BO-PEEP

ugly son. But I have heard the fairies say that one day a lovely maiden, who would come into this wood to find her lost sheep, should be the means of my gaining my own form again. You are that pretty maid, and I will take you to a spot where you will find your sheep, but without their tails. The elves will play with them for this night, but in the morning every sheep will have its tail again,

Joseph Martin Kronheim

LITTLE BO-PEEP

except the stupid Bell-wether.
You must then wave his tail three
times over my head, and I shall
resume my shape again."

The owl flew off, and led Bo-Peep
into the wood, and said, "Sleep,
maiden, I will watch." How long
she was asleep she could not tell,
but the charmed spot was suddenly
lighted up, and she saw the Queen
of the Fairies seated on a bank.
The Queen said the sheep should

Joseph Martin Kronheim

be punished for running away. She then saw all her sheep come trooping into the place, and on every sheep there was an Elf, who held in his hand a sheep's tail.

Joseph Martin Kronheim

LITTLE BO-PEEP

Joseph Martin Kronheim

LITTLE BO-PEEP

After riding them about for some
time, and having great fun with
them, the mad sport ceased, and
each Elf restored the tail to his
sheep—all but the Bell-wether's,
which their leader hid in a tree.
When Bo-Peep awoke, she saw
the owl flapping its wings as if to
remind her of her promise; so she
fetched the tail, and waved it
three times over its head, when up
started the most charming Princess

Joseph Martin Kronheim

that ever was seen. The princess
gave Bo-Peep a beautiful cottage,
and her sheep never ran away from
their kind mistress again.

Joseph Martin Kronheim

LITTLE BO-PEEP

Joseph Martin Kronheim

End of the book.

Joseph Martin Kronheim

www.ingramcontent.com/pod-product-compliance
Lightning Source LLC
Chambersburg PA
CBHW070123010626
45794CB00012B/1250